BRAVING THE
BIG FREEZE

BookLife PUBLISHING

©2023
BookLife Publishing Ltd.
King's Lynn, Norfolk
PE30 4LS, UK

A catalogue record for this book is available from the British Library.

ISBN: 978-1-80505-021-6

Written by:
Madeline Tyler
Adapted by:
Sam Thompson
Edited by:
Kirsty Holmes
Designed by:
Amy Li

All facts, statistics, web addresses and URLs in this book were verified as valid and accurate at time of writing. No responsibility for any changes to external websites or references can be accepted by either the author or publisher.

FSC
www.fsc.org
MIX
Paper from responsible sources
FSC® C113515

AN INTRODUCTION TO BOOKLIFE RAPID READERS...

Packed full of gripping topics and twisted tales, BookLife Rapid Readers are perfect for older children looking to propel their reading up to top speed. With three levels based on our planet's fastest animals, children will be able to find the perfect point from which to accelerate their reading journey. From the spooky to the silly, these roaring reads will turn every child at every reading level into a prolific page-turner!

CHEETAH

The fastest animals on land, cheetahs will be taking their first strides as they race to top speed.

MARLIN

The fastest animals under water, marlins will be blasting through their journey.

FALCON

The fastest animals in the air, falcons will be flying at top speed as they tear through the skies.

Photo Credits – Images are courtesy of Shutterstock.com. With thanks to Getty Images, Thinkstock Photo and iStockphoto. Recurring images – mycteria, benchart, Andrii_Malysh, Bohdan Populov, Anastasiia Veretennikova, Francois Poirier. Cover – Zerbor, jakkapan, nayuki minase. 4–5 – Esteban De Armas, FedBul. 6–7 – Aunt Spray, Rashevskyi Viacheslav, Yaroslav Vitkovskiy. 8–9 – Bluemoon 1981, Lisina Margarita, Mathias Berlin. 10–11 – Africa Studio, ibrahim Buraganov, Sambulov Yevgeniy. 12–13 – Maximillian cabinet, PrimeMockup, Salienko Evgenii, Volodymyr Baleha. 14–15 – ChiccoDodiFC, FabrikaSimf, mady70, Vereshchagin Dmitry. 16–17 – Bianca Grueneberg, Picture Partners, solarseven, Valery Evlakhov. 18–19 – ALIAKSANDR BUTRYM, andreiuc88, 20–21 – Dziurek, high fliers. 22–23 – Alexandre Laprise, e-leet. 24–25 – nasim.shikdar, GenadijsZ. 26–27 – Lysogor Roman, Vixit. 28–29 – Dmitry Molchanov, Marti Bug Catcher.

CONTENTS

Words that look like this are explained in the glossary on page 31.

THE BIG FREEZE

Do you like the cold? What about snow? How does a world covered in ice sound to you?

The ground becomes white. Then, it starts to get chilly. Soon, your feet are stuck in a layer of ice.

IT IS AN ICE AGE...

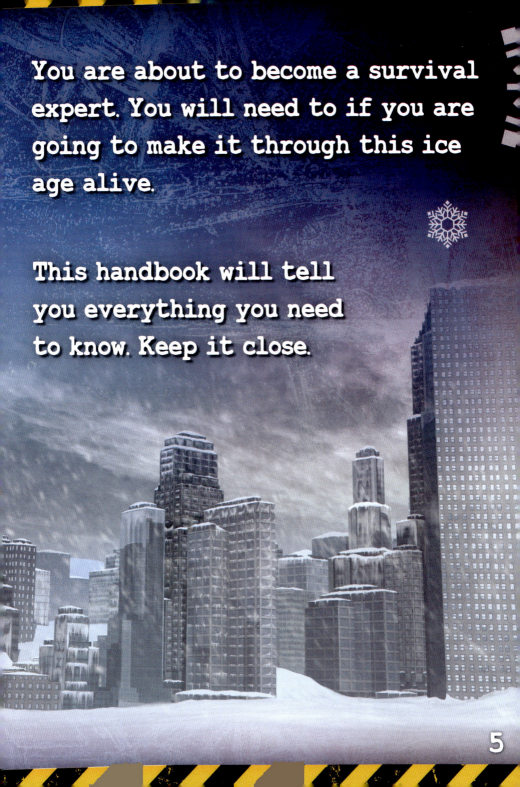

You are about to become a survival expert. You will need to if you are going to make it through this ice age alive.

This handbook will tell you everything you need to know. Keep it close.

NOT THE FIRST
NOR THE LAST

This is not the first ice age. It will not be the last, either. There have been five ice ages so far.

The last one was 10,000 years ago. Some animals died. Others <u>adapted</u> to survive.

The woolly mammoths, sabre-toothed cats and cave bears went <u>extinct</u>.

Yet humans survived. Now, you will have to do it again.

Wrap up warm, it is going to be a chilly ride...

ABOVE AND BELOW

LOOK OUT! The Sun has been covered by clouds. Those clouds are more dangerous than they seem.

They drop giant hailstones because of the freezing cold weather. Find something to protect your head!

This is not what you mean, is it?

The dangers do not just come from above. An ice age means one thing: ice! Outside your window is a giant glacier.

Glaciers are huge chunks of ice that move like slow, frozen rivers. You will need to find some cover, and soon.

WHAT DO YOU MEAN, 'WARM'?

It is time to find somewhere warmer. Grab your stuff and start to trek away from the glacier.

Find a buddy to pair up with. It might be difficult to see in the blizzards.

We are heading for the Equator. This is a made-up line that runs around the middle of the Earth like a belt.

It is the warmest part of the Earth. Right now, it is your safest bet.

WARNING!
It will still be freezing at the Equator!

Equator

Are you at the Equator?
Good. Keep reading...

You need to start digging a <u>bunker</u> straight away. Choose your spot wisely. You will be here for a few years at least.

Is Grandma too tired? It does not matter. Everyone must dig NOW!

EMERGENCY BACKUP PLAN

If you cannot dig, follow these steps…

Step 1: Find a mountain.

Step 2: Locate a cave.

Step 3: Check it is free of bears.

Step 4: Collect dry wood nearby.

Step 5: Light a fire for warmth.

EQUIP YOURSELF

You need some important equipment to help you survive. Snowshoes are a must-have. They will stop you sinking in the snow.

Keep a shovel close by. You will need it to clear the way. Just do not spend too long outside.

Cover as much of your body as you can with clothes. Layers are important. The more you have, the warmer you will be.

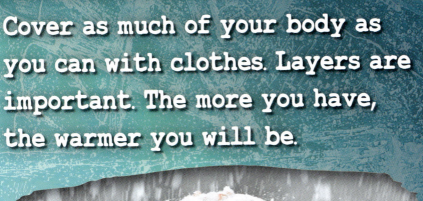

Collect jumpers, coats and blankets whenever you see them!

If you had been prepared, you would have packed some <u>fire starters</u>.

No matter. You can use your matches to start a fire. If your fire gets out of control, use your shovel to dump some snow on it.

The fire can also be used to cook food and warm up drinks. Stock your hideout with plenty of food.

Canned food will last the longest.

How do you find food, I hear you ask? Turn the page...

FINDING FOOD

If your greedy brother has already gobbled up all the food, read on.

You may have to learn about <u>foraging</u>, fishing and hunting to keep your family alive. Be brave. It will be tough out there!

Most plants will have been killed off by the ice outside. If you are lucky, you might find some nuts, seeds or berries left over.

WATCH OUT!
Always take an adult if you go out foraging. Some berries are <u>poisonous</u>.

Have the berries and nuts run out? You might have to learn to hunt like the people in the last ice age did.

You and your crew will need a bow and arrow. Stick together and take your shot. You cannot afford to miss!

No part of your catch should go to waste. Store any extra meat in ice to keep it fresh.

You can use bones to make tools such as spears. The fur can be used to make a warm coat, too.

Have you lived long enough
to see the Sun come back?
You have? Excellent!

The ice will begin to melt and
the rivers will begin to flow
again. The ice age is not over yet,
but at least the fish are back.

That means more food! Try perching on a rock to get a good view into the water.

You will have to stand very still and then be very quick with your spear. Be careful. Falling into the icy water could spell the end for you!

DISASTER AFTER
DISASTER

The snow and ice will continue to melt. That means you might notice a lot more water around.

The sea levels will rise and the land will begin to flood. It is time to swap your snowshoes for some wellies... and a snorkel.

Towns and cities will be under deep water in a short while. You must find a boat any way you can.

If you are out of luck, head for high ground. Once again, mountains are your backup plan!

Mountains come with their own dangers. The melting snow and ice could begin to break away from the mountains.

It may fall in giant chunks, moving very fast down the sides. This is called an avalanche.

Avalanches can cause serious damage. If you hear the rumble of an avalanche, move quickly.

Keep your eyes peeled, too. A large white cloud of snow will tell you that an avalanche is just seconds away!

Did the avalanche make it down to the sea? No? Thank goodness for that. You could have been in the path of a giant wave.

These waves are bigger than you could ever imagine. They would wipe out everything in their path.

That should be the last test. If you are still reading this, you are a real-life superhero. The fate of humanity rests on you.

Look for survivors. Group together. Without each other, nobody will make it through.

CHECKLIST

How to brave the big freeze:

- ☐ Find a helmet.
- ☐ Head to the Equator.
- ☐ Dig or find a cave.
- ☐ Make a fire.
- ☐ Find food.
- ☐ Collect clothes.
- ☐ Find a boat or get to high ground.

GLOSSARY

ADAPTED   changed over time to suit the environment

BUNKER   reinforced underground shelter

EXTINCT   when a species of animal is no longer alive

FIRE STARTERS   pieces of flammable material used to start a fire

FORAGING   searching for food

POISONOUS   dangerous or deadly when eaten

INDEX